O is for Obedience

Dr. C. White-Elliott
Illustrated by Ariana Halverson

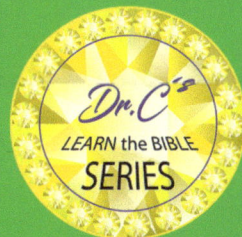

www.clfpublishing.org
909.315.3161

Cover design by Senir Design. Contact info: info@senirdesign.com

Illustrated by Ariana Halverson AHalver3rs0n@gmail.com

ISBN #978-1-945102-64-6

Printed in the United States of America.

Dedicated to

London McFarquhar

"Children, obey your parents in the Lord, for this is right."

Ephesians 6:1

Kamper the kangaroo likes to play practical jokes on everyone, including his parents and his little brother and older sister. His parents understand their middle child and his love of jokes. However, they want to make sure he understands how to follow directions and rules. So, they teach him a few things about obedience.

The first lesson Kamper's parents teach him is to keep his room clean as one of his chores. Kamper must clean his room every day after school.

On Monday, when Kamper returns home from school, he places his backpack on the kitchen counter. He grabs a snack and heads over to the couch to play his favorite video game. His mother instructs him to first complete his homework because he needs to have strong reading, writing and math skills.

Kamper goes to his bedroom, sits at his desk, and takes his books from his backpack. For the next hour, he completes the assignments his teachers gave him. He reads, he writes, and he completes his math problems. He is obedient because he follows his mother's and teachers' instructions.

After Kamper completes his homework, he enjoys his video games. A little while later, his father is in the kitchen making dinner. He calls out to Kamper to come assist him with dinner. At first, Kamper complains. When he sees the look of disappointment in his father's eyes, he does as his father asks.

On Saturday afternoon, Kamper and his little brother Kooper play outside in the backyard. Kooper decides to jump into a muddy puddle. When their mother sees how dirty Kooper is, she asks Kamper to take Kooper inside to give him a bath.

One of Kooper's bath toys is a rubber snake that looks lifelike. Kamper thinks it's a good idea to prank their big sister Korsella. Quietly, he tips into her bedroom and places the rubber snake on her pillow. A few minutes later, Korsella enters the room and sees the toy. She screams and runs from the room and stubs her toe in the doorway. She yells. When their mother finds out what happened, she tells Kamper to apologize to Korsella.

On Sunday, Kamper and Kooper toss the ball around in the backyard. The ball goes into the neighbor's yard. Kamper jumps over the fence to get it. His mother sees him and tells him it is disrespectful to enter another person's private property without permission. He goes to the neighbor's front door and asks for the ball.

Did Kamper do a good job of learning how to obey? Do you obey your parents?

Children, remember it is important to obey what your parents tell you because they are preparing you to deal with real life.

www.ingramcontent.com/pod-product-compliance
Lightning Source LLC
Chambersburg PA
CBHW041957100426
42813CB00019B/2912